Sharmistha Mohanty is the author of three works of prose, *Book One*, *New Life*, and *Five Movements in Praise*. She has also translated a selection of Rabindranath Tagore's fiction, *Broken Nest and Other Stories*. Her prose and poetry have appeared in several journals, including *Granta*, *Poetry*, *World Literature Today*, and *The Caravan*.

Mohanty is the founder editor of the *Almost Island* project which includes an online journal, the *Almost Island Dialogues* series—an annual international writers meet—and the publication of books.

She was on the International Faculty for the Creative Writing MFA at the City University of Hong Kong for several years.

She lives in Mumbai.

ALSO BY SHARMISTHA MOHANTY

Book One (1995)

New Life (2005)

Broken Nest and Other Stories by Rabindranath Tagore (trans.) (2009)

Five Movements in Praise (2013)

PRAISE FOR *FIVE MOVEMENTS IN PRAISE*

'[*Five Movements*] is an intricate, idiosyncratic masterpiece which demands to be read solely on its own terms.'
—*The Sunday Guardian*

'Creative prose is at its most beautiful meticulousness here, turning every little detail into a lasting image and every encounter with men, women and objects into a moment of epiphany.'

—K. Satchidanandan, *Frontline*

'Sharmistha Mohanty is a clear and present example of the writer as caver, her work a descent into rock in pursuit of a shape half known and calling. It's not surprising that her touchstone is the great temple at Ellora. Her reader moves with something of the excitement of the soldier who discovered that series of caves when out hunting, but the author's stance is that of the first sculptor as he paused on the volcanic outcrop to imagine his way down into the living rock.'

—I. Allan Sealy

'Sharmistha Mohanty is remarkable above all for her determination to shift narrative away from the easy urgencies of Western fiction towards a text that hovers between the contemplative and the hypnotic... To read *Five Movements* is like coming across an animal of a new species, but one that immediately appears to be in tune with its environment.'

—Tim Parks

The Gods Came Afterwards

Poems

Sharmistha Mohanty

SPEAKING TIGER PUBLISHING PVT. LTD
4381/4, Ansari Road, Daryaganj
New Delhi 110002

First published in hardback by Speaking Tiger 2019

Copyright © Sharmistha Mohanty 2019

ISBN: 978-93-89231-69-4
eISBN: 978-93-89231-68-7

10 9 8 7 6 5 4 3 2 1

The moral right of the author has been asserted.

All rights reserved.
No part of this publication may be reproduced, transmitted, or stored in a retrieval system, in any form or by any means, electronic, mechanical, photocopying, recording or otherwise, without the prior permission of the publisher.

This book is sold subject to the condition that it shall not, by way of trade or otherwise, be lent, resold, hired out, or otherwise circulated, without the publisher's prior consent in any form of binding or cover other than that in which it is published.

For

Anna Deeny Morales, prescient friend

Contents

Make broadness broadness / 1

Give us powerful force / 3

Bring bring us / 5

Take take us / 6

Take take us, lead lead us / 7

May we live / 8

I make myself broad / 9

The mountain passes / 10

Broadness being / 11

A snake eats a mynah / 12

Granaries as long / 14

The world gathered / 16

Fire, the trembler / 17

The clearing I / 18

Rising, the falcon folds / 19

Far through mountain passes / 21

Unclose the nights / 23

From the time / 24

Lead us towards / 25

Undeniable what was / 27

The unlocatable solitary / 28

Take us / 29

Bearing light in the mouth / 30

Without looking back / 31

Looking back / 33

Us, crowded together / 34

Wide wide give us / 35

No images made in stone / 37

The narrow moves / 38

Who comes through fire / 39

Memory in the mouth / 40

Voracious the void / 41

Mornings of bronze / 42

Paddy fields / 43

The pupil dilates / 44

These scorched feet / 45

Bring us near nearer / 46

Because the world / 48

Past beyond perception / 49

Core of darkness / 50

Alluvial broadness / 51

What is and what is not yet / 52

Falcon spreads his wings / 54

Hold us / 55

What can never / 56

Give us / 57

This here / 58

In the sudden burst of fire / 59

I can see the earth / 61

What shall I / 62

Lengthen our breath / 63

The river winds far / 64

Iron from breaking stars / 65

A leopard / 66

Nothing / 68

Not the history / 69

Still rising / 71

When the fires / 72

Glossary of Sanskrit Words / 74

Notes / 75

Acknowledgements / 77

Make broadness broadness
from narrowness
Lead lead us
We see nothing
behind nothing ahead
These worlds are broad above
beyond our knowing
The great river plains open and descend
slowly from west to east
beyond our knowing
Us
Doctor, suture me from
narrowness to broadness
All the suns all the dawns all the waters
rise and pass
in broadness
Our bodies move over over this land
rising and falling
Broadness
stretch out our skies and dawns
so we can walk walk

out of ourselves

Doctor, move me from dark

spaces of invented light

I do not know just

what it is

that I am like

Broadness open for

us us

Unharness our days

Let all boundaries be distant

so we can wander far

in our unknowing

Give us powerful
force
give give us the power
of our conquerors
take us
where hope and broadness
meet
like the tributaries
of a river

What shall I say
what shall I think?

Take take us
towards a thousand unrisen
dawns
give us knowledge
of what what
is and
is to be
do not exile us

from immensity

may we see

the earth

at a single glance

and

in all its details

Bring bring us
let let us
us
bring us longer winters like
this one
when nothing withers
when evening comes early
may we be like
the earth
predictable and free
assure assure us
I know your heart
earth
that rests in the skies
I know your heart
may it know
me

Take take us
take us
us
the bleeding barn owl
unmoving
in the bell tower next
to the rusted bell
the injured evening
the alcoholic behind
flowered curtains
threatening his mother
with death
take us to a broad
world
far flung earth, bright
one
where we can
see
let all light reach
its destiny

Take take us
lead lead us
keep keep us
let let us
give give us
bring bring us

May we live

may we see

may we rise

from our sources

may we become

may we

I make myself broad
                out of narrowness
I make broadness from
                narrowness
Doctor, the long, long scar
                grows dim
so also your hands that
                opened me
to the knowing
                of uncertainty
maker of paths
                on sky and earth
take us
                across the scarred forests

―――――――

The mountain passes are closing in
                do not exile us from light
untethered galaxies
untethered truth
                light
may we see the difference in
every new dawn
                light
what is in the heart is also near is also difference
is also another
                light
the earth though broad has
become narrow
                light
the eyes of tree cutters
the stump of a flowering tree
the stump of a man
                light
may these sloping river plains be
without conclusion
                light
lead us past what pursues us
                do not exile us from light

Broadness

       being

broadness

       becoming

broadness

       all that is moving and still

broadness

       origin

broadness

       containing
       brimming
       spilling

broadness

       unflinching

A snake eats a mynah
head first, yellow legs extend
from the snake's filled mouth
the cattle bellow
tethered to ancient trees
dung fills the tall grass
thunder strikes at the humid air
there is no I
in the breath
roots wind through fallen leaves
the terror of an owl smashes
into a tree trunk, loses a wing,
drops below into dried weeds
there is no I
in the breath
the seasons are muscular and original
what should I
speak
thunder strikes again and again
what is real must be harvested
each day and threshed and ground

put through fire

then eaten

what should I

imagine

in this place where we become

our sight is made

from our seasons

bring us

the rain

Granaries as long
and winding as
the shores from
which we look
at the lit ocean, behind
us the fertile land, rivers
coming to this sea, silt
behind us thousands
of years
the vertebrae compressed
the spine bending
forward forever
behind us
offerings of fire held
in falcons with outstretched
wings, built brick by brick
flight
abandoned, vanished
in unpredictable encounters
before us rusted barges
the daily fragrance
of spices in oil

a fatigued infinity of sea and sky

what can I

go towards

remote acts

fires kindled on

empty clearings, sloping

towards the east

chanted word

vigilant thought

dispersed

astral distance wedged

in the spinal cord

behind us a broad land grown

narrow

at its very end

The world gathered in the pupil

of an eye

the boundless plain filled with scars

earth stretching on and on

measuring out distances

of desire

making a clearing

being present at the meeting axis

of earth and sky

can I

even now

correct the course of things

Fire, the trembler
fire, the praiser
   the praised
fire, giver and scorcher
   of sight
fire,
   forever forward
   opening the way

Forming the ground
   in the life breath
laying the mind
   in the life breath
offering the fire
   there

The clearing I

I the fire-kindler and the fire I

the animal untied and led away and choked

the offering I

I the hand and breath that stretches and extends I

the ground of the universe

Rising, the falcon folds
his large wings
stained by matter all
the way behind him
ten thousand eight hundred
bricks
that made him
begin to split and fall
raising both his wings
high above his head
he pushes up
leaves earth
soil and sand
come down breaking
the shadow of his form
below
water drips down from
the falcon's body
and milk then ash
dispersing into the air
then the things that must come
unstuck

The Gods Came Afterwards

stalks of grass, straw, bits

of plants

leaving this falling offering

behind

the falcon flies towards

the east

bird of farthest sight

being of swiftest flight

travelling between narrowness

and broadness

for there is no third

travelling through what

is propped

apart

on the ground all

that the falcon has shed

debris, smoke

the offering's breath

broadness broadness

spreading, leaving

behind the carcass

of narrowness

Far through mountain
passes onto the sloping
river plains land
opening, stretching on
moving, settling
over and over
suturing the fatal wound
at the navel of
the universe
over and over
memorizing both
the blood that spills
and the healer's hands
far three thousand years
forming metre forming
gesture forming sight
building nothing
in stone
moving forward
with what moves
systole and diastole

not leaving everything
to thought alone
grasping tools
kindling fire
growing lighter breath
by breath
can I
even now
make new
the born
of old?

Unclose
the nights
unbind
our thoughts
give us an
uncircumscribed
earth
make us of
broad gaze

From the time

when time

was measured by

a bird's wings

memory

stained by ash and milk and

rivers wide

as seas

by rust and honey and

jealousy

by *haldi* and blood and

wonder

by wood shavings and spittle and

anguish

by crushed barley and smoke and

distances waiting

by dung and flames and

insight

by boiled rice and horse's hooves and

vengeance

memory unslayable

Lead us towards
the better
thing
sharpen these
songs
I ask you about the farthest ends of the earth
I ask where is the navel of the living world
might I reach
the broad light
that is free
of fear
let the long darkness not
reach us
speech wanders between
the two worlds
let not the full measure
of my work be
broken
before its season
unfasten from me
fear
sharpen

these songs

like an axe

with a whetstone

release from us

even the guilt

that we create

conceal the concealable

darkness

run over every

rapacious one

make the light

that we

desire

Undeniable

what was

blown in from

elsewhere by

the wind like

seeds with wings

or pushing up

from this earth

like water

it was

do not exile us

from remembering

―――――――――

The unlocatable

solitary

in the highest

mountains like

a plant

a stone

a pool

like

the ravine

below

Take us
to the origins
of a thing
may it be
unreliable
or far
what we can
scarcely see
colliding
with what we
each day
touch
the origin
of water
in the forming
of stars

Bearing light in
the mouth
I light a syllable
and all the other
syllables follow
I light the springtime
and all the other
seasons follow
With my labour
I illuminate
ancient things
bearing light
in the mouth
at night's
boundary

Without looking back
she yokes her thoughts
she digests the fire
and walks away

Without looking back
she leaves behind the cattle
she leaves behind the ripening barley
and walks away

Without looking back
she leaves her life
she leaves narrowness
and walks away

Without looking back
she leaves behind anyone who calls
she leaves behind her implements
and walks away

Without looking back
she springs from a metaphor
she becomes real
and walks away

Without looking back
she springs from the real
she becomes a metaphor
and walks away

Looking back
is inauspicious
looking back
is the axe
not sharpened

Us, crowded

together

in humid darkness

like soil

lengthen our

lifetimes

the wet green hills

grow evening black

the lamp flames

truth's veracity bends

gutters, rises

darkness stays still

saliva drips from

the god's outstretched

tongue

Wide wide

give us

a wide unwavering

earth

where we can

become

we who try

to be

wakeful

always

who stays awake

him

the light desires

who stays awake

him

all the worlds desire

how many worlds

are there

always more than

one

and never fewer than

two

turn

towards towards

us

all the worlds

turn the earth

away

from those we

hate

and from those

who hate

us

turn towards

towards us

the winds

the waters

us

turn us

towards

No images made
in stone no
shrines no chronicles
of lost times
eight months
of unclouded sight
four months
of rain to
clarify light
each day
broadness
forming in the pupil
of an eye

The narrow moves
with us always
anguish stays close
stays the course
while we thresh
the invisible things

Who comes through
fire shines in
ashes
quiet and lucid
as the embers
that glow beneath

Memory in the mouth
moistened by saliva
mending the moment
breath by breath
saying saying
syllable by syllable
making, meaning
mind in the mouth
moving tongue
against teeth
remembering rhythms
invoking, impelling
increasing
fighting fate
marking the mystery

Voracious the void

tenacious our trust

vital our verses

tenuous our truth

taste and touch

vision and voice

treading the tilt of time

tangible the terrain

tendril twig tree

vigilant our vision

vanquished our victories

thoughtful the tribe

truthful the thunder

Mornings of bronze

twilights of copper

iron nights

staying of metal

passing of light

Paddy fields

earth marked by ploughs

us, us

wedding fire

scattered seeds

us, us

line of spiders moving

lines from then to now

crossing the ground

of time

us, us

warp and weft

twisted rope

us, us

scales of fish

flowers of dung

us, us

crescent moon

garland of leaves

us, us

The pupil dilates
in darkness
to discern
the undiscernable

origins of things
the moving glint
of precise cause
why a meteorite

hits the earth
why we receive the
debris of the universe
why the flawed

act the disfigured
feeling the contorted
heart the rinds and
skins of being

release us from explanation

These scorched

feet

this slow walk around

fire

these palms skimming

flames

this being

witnessed

this undispersed

ground

this unexhausted

circle

this unrigid

truth

this unstone this

fire

this slow centripetal

force

―――――――

Bring us near nearer

not further far

take us close closer

unbuild us

to soil gravel mud

fold back the excess

of cloth so we

may weave again

unmake us

a nocturnal sorrow

opens

over the great river plains

the falcon with a

single wing

flies alongside

move us from unfire

to fire

return stone

to the mountains

unfirm us

the alcoholic stoops low

on his plastic stool

in the middle
of the precarious alleyway
unsure our voices
so we can listen
sometimes
make us many
the not-one
and only then
make us one
the not-two
take us away from
calculations
so there remain only
near and distant
high and low
early and late
para and *avara*
the front and the back
and the four
directions

Because the world is
neither fixed or
provisional
neither new or
repeated
neither certainty or
chance
hold your palms side
by side
as for a drink of water

Past beyond

perception

what has already

become

a rotating

now

what is likely

to be

what has not yet

come

Core of darkness

covered

by darkness

what stirs

core of light

covered

by light

what moves back

and forth

what was

uncertain

at the beginning

remains uncertain

at the end

Alluvial broadness
bearing great river plains
spreading in the slow
thoughts of animals
that graze converging
in the perfect speed
of the predator's
chase beginning at
each instant
this ancient of days
at every moment
the universe at stake
broadness flooding plains
the river's wide mouth
repeating what is always
unprecedented

What is and
what is not yet
travel towards
each other
deflected
sometimes by the
turning
of the earth
corrected
in their course
by an animate
grammar
abhaya
travelling away from
fear
akrodh
traveling away from
anger
advaya
travelling towards
another

grammar of searching

From darkness

lead

From untruth

move

Falcon spreads his wings

after rain

sits still under

sun's light

as clouds pass

again

he folds his wings in

waits

for light to return

Hold us

in nearest nearness

sharpen our weapons

so we can wound

those whose speech and hands

are empty

those who turn the truth

assure us

though there is no

assurance

take us

to our desires

urgent like thirst

patient like earth

smasher of the unluminous

of brutal contradictions

joy maker

us

What can never

be repaired

it was never

broken

what can never

be broken

it was not

built

what can never

be stitched

it was never torn

what never

needed a spine

invertebrate

and everywhere

Give us

the power

to be undermined

to become ash

calm the anxiety in

our hands

make them precise

so the axe comes

down on wood not

flowers

so we can hold

two opposed feelings

of equal weight

repeat the unexhausted

space

that carries far

a human cry

This here

this

not some other

place this

not beyond

this now

not before

or after

In the sudden
burst of fire
in the slowness
of ashes
in the space between
inhalation and
exhalation
in the syllables
that are still
unscathed
in all that has
fallen
become part
of the earth's core
dark *ksham*
in the light from
the sky
moving us forward
in the water that
carries away what is
broken forever

in the hand opening
towards the flame
the lightest things
last

I can see

the earth I'm

looking at

the clouds

beautiful, so

beautiful

I can see

the earth's

horizon

it has a beautiful

blue halo

the sky is

black

I can see

stars[1]

---

[1] The words of Yuri Gagarin from space. He was the first person to orbit the earth.

———————

What shall I

say

what shall I

think

can I

even now

I ask

where

what should I

imagine

what can I

go towards

Lengthen our breath
make it slow slow
on its way
us made of panic
and lustre
us
working against
the unmade
making
against the height
of the hills the mass
of the mountains the spread
of the seas the length
of the land
against ourselves

The river winds far
further than dread
can travel
the rocks at the shore
are basalt formed
a million years
ago longer than
panic can look
for its source

Iron from breaking
stars
iron from earthly
blood
remains of melted
meteorites
the navel of a man
all that comes
from the navel of the
universe
turning the earth
holder of more than
everything
matter and fate
melted down
the end of the
unfinished
things coming from
very far very far
and very near very near
light and the
warp and weft of days
turning the earth
turning the earth

A leopard watches
the city
at night when roads
and homes are made
of light
his night vision reaching
the city's end the
dark grieving sea seen
from the denuded
hills of his hunger
above
the international space station
brightest thing
in the night sky after
the moon
is stalking the turning
earth hunting down
the mysteries of the
universe
below
someone clearing the earth
clearing the earth

trying to

clear the earth

of an immense hunger for

everything

someone trying

to begin

―――――――――

Nothing not
infinite

Nothing that can
be grown
or severed

Nothing that has
intention

Not knowledge
not power

Not the history of
a life
never what is
personal
always what is
outside time
never a moment that
begins
to end
never a life and
a horizon
never all lines meeting
far away
no hope to be
fulfilled
always a returning like
the turning earth
never an arrow moving
forward
never a receding
far

always an emerging
forth
this invariable face
this variable body
a whole not
a consequence
but an impulse
from where everything
begins
never things one
at a time
but a manifold
universe
how many suns are there
how many dawns
how many waters
the universe in a child's
opened mouth
not muscle or sinew
nothing to resist
the precision of
infinity

Still rising these mountains
still moving this land
slowly northeast
still tectonic
its breath

When the fires
can no longer
be seen
someone has walked
far enough
the bird that
eats
and the bird that
watches
the bird that
eats
are both silent
in night's impure black
the paths into the forest
are charred
their length invented
by the feet that walk
to be away to
be awake to be
no one

Glossary of Sanskrit Words

para and *avara*: far and near
abhaya: non-fear
akrodha: non-anger
advaya: the not-two
ksham: soil

Notes

One of the inspirations for this book was the Rig Veda, which historians date from approximately 1200-900 BCE. From that inspiration, along with others, these poems have charted their own course. The Rig Veda is the oldest religious and spiritual text still in use and it forms the basis of what was later called Hinduism. At the time when the Rig Vedic hymns were composed there was a belief that new hymns must continually be made for use in rituals and worship. And in fact the hymns were composed over hundreds of years by various poets and seers and passed down orally. It was only much later that these became the canon and nothing new was added. Around 1200 CE the hymns were collated, written down and composed into a text.

Pg. 2, I do not know just what/it is/that I am like, RV, 1.164

Pg. 4, May we see/the earth/at a single glance/and/in all its details, RV 10.158

Pg. 5, I know your heart/earth/that rests in the skies/I know your heart/may it know/me
Amended version of lines from the Paraksara Grihya Sutra, 1.16.7

Pg. 9, I make myself broad/out of narrowness
Amended version of the RV 2.26.4

Pg. 18, Reference to a Vedic ritual where an animal is sacrificed by choking it

Pg. 19, This poem refers to the Agnicayana ritual practised in Vedic times roughly 3,000 years ago, where an immense prayer altar is made from bricks in the shape of a falcon or eagle. It is occasionally still performed

Pg. 25, This poem is composed of unrelated fragments culled from the RV

Pg. 30, With my labour/I illuminate/ancient things, RV 3.55.289

Pg. 51, This ancient of days, Atharva Veda, 7.21

Pg. 53, From darkness lead/from untruth move, Brhadaranyaka Upanisads, 1.3.28

Pg. 70, How many suns are there/how many dawns/how many waters, RV 10.88.18

English translations of the Rig Veda consulted here are by Raimundo Panikkar, Wendy Doniger O'Flaherty, Stephanie Jamison and Joel Brereton

Acknowledgements

For the lifegivers, Dr Hemant Tongaonkar and Dr Vinita Salvi, for their gifted hands and singular compassion.

For the healers, Father Joe Pereira and Dr Dayal Mirchandani and the worlds they opened.

For Dr N.R. Hingorani and Dr Mihir Patki for their careful attention to the everyday.

For Raúl Zurita, illuminator, who shone a light through the dark spaces on poetry and endurance, on poetry's endurance.

For Anamika Haksar, beloved friend, in whose sight and deep companionship these poems found strength.

For Rahul Soni whose eye for detail and patient support were always at hand.

For my closest friends—they know who they are—for being *there*.

For Munir and Subhashis who came.

And for K, unflickering, like a lamp in a windless place.

Selections from these poems have appeared in *Poetry*, *World Literature Today*, *The Indian Quarterly* and *Guftugu*. The very first poem, *Make broadness broadness*, was a text, light and sound installation at the Kochi-Muziris Biennale 2016-17, curated by Sudarshan Shetty.

www.ingramcontent.com/pod-product-compliance
Lightning Source LLC
Chambersburg PA
CBHW070309240426
43663CB00039BA/2554